MORE MANLY PRAISE FOR

DUDE TO DAD

"Few parenting books have been as honest, funny, and true as this look at what happens to a man the moment he becomes a dad! Sure, there have been thousands written about the moms of the world, but finally the male side of the parenting coin is getting the attention it deserves!"

—C.C. Chapman, Dad and Author of *Amazing Things Will Happen*

"There are dozens of baby books out there to choose from. There are very few dad books. And none of them provide the useful insight and hilarious honesty offered in *Dude To Dad: The First 9 Months*. As a future dad, I plan to keep this book glued to my hand at all times. It may not make fatherhood easy, but it will certainly make it a little less terrifying."

—Mike Billeter, Dude and Author of *Samuel Sporter, the Bravest Reporter*

DUDE TO DAD

DUDE TO DAD

THE FIRST 9 MONTHS

BY HUGH WEBER, WITH MRS. DUDE AND EMERSON

familius

Published by Familius LLC, www.familius.com

Familius books are available at special discounts for bulk
purchases for sales promotions, family, or corporate use.
Special editions, including personalized covers, excerpts
of existing books, or books with corporate logos, can be
created in large quantities for special needs. For more
information, contact Premium Sales at 559-876-2170 or email
specialmarkets@familius.com.

pISBN 978-1-938301-26-1
eISBN 978-1-938301-25-4
Library of Congress Control Number 2013933810

Printed in the United States of America

Book design by David Miles
Jacket design by David Miles
Edited by Preston Wittwer

10 9 8 7 6 5 4 3 2 1

First Edition

To Roscoe & Jimmy, who set unreasonably high standards for the dads that would follow.

To Mrs. Dude, your patience was (and is) commendable, and your baby-making skills—extraordinary!

CONTENTS

PROLOGUE

STAGE ONE: BEFORE BIRTH

STAGE TWO: BIRTH

STAGE THREE: AFTERBIRTH

"THE SURPR
ABOUT FATH
FINDING MY
NOW I WANT
WITH THE

ISING THING
ERHOOD WAS
INNER MUSH.
TO SHARE IT
WORLD."

—Christopher Meloni

PROLOGUE

You've seen the photos before, right? I had seen dozens of them over the past couple years. Brothers, college hallmates, and Facebook friends that I don't even recognize, all striking the same pose.

Screaming baby just minutes removed from the womb. Beaming fathers triumphant with the successful transmission of their genetic code. A cross-generational meeting without complication. Pure, uninhibited joy.

Or so I thought.

What I didn't see was the culmination of nine months of self-doubt and anxiety intersecting with the beginning of a journey of even more mystery, intrigue, and confusion. I didn't realize that each of those men, regardless of circumstances, was in the middle of a mystifying and magical transition from Dude to Dad.

I was on the ultimate dude trip when I first found out that I was going to be a father. We had just landed on a dirt runway in the Arctic Ocean off the north slope of Alaska. I picked up the satellite phone to call my wife and let her know we had survived the most aggressive part of the trip. She told me that she thought she should take "the test."

Six days later, we sat in our bedroom waiting for the test to share the results and I found myself mindlessly repeating "holy crap, holy crap, holy crap" as it came up positive.

Little did I know that the transition had just begun.

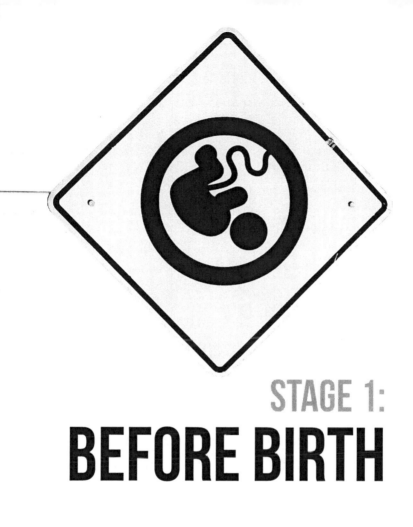

BEFORE BIRTH

For the sake of simplicity, I'm going to assume that you know how you got here. Becoming a father, my friend, was an exciting and engaging exercise. Congratulations on a job well done.

But those ninety seconds are over. This isn't a how-to manual and that's not why you're here anyway, is it?

You, no doubt, have come to the realization that you are a simple Dude that

<u>d</u>idn't

<u>u</u>nderstand

<u>d</u>aunting

<u>e</u>xpectations

before this recent fatherhood turn. Your hope (or perhaps the hope of the person who bought this book . . . Hi Mom!) is that someone or something can help you make the transition from Dude to a

<u>d</u>edicated

<u>an</u>d

<u>d</u>etermined

Dad.

Despite your enthusiasm, chances are good that this book, despite its brief and bite-sized nature, won't be read in full until it's too late. With that in mind, I'm going to cut straight to the most important thing for you to know.

1. EVERYTHING HAS CHANGED.

Let me say it again for proper emphasis.

EVERYTHING HAS CHANGED.

It's neither good, nor bad. It just is.

What's changed, you ask? Everything.

Everything? Everything.

Many a man before you has spent months and even years fighting this one simple truth. There's this sense that if you wait it out or power through, that things will return to "normal." The plain and simple truth is that there is a new normal . . . and everything has changed.

If you can accept this in all of its excitements and disappointments, you are going to be that much closer to making the transition from Dude to Dad.

2. ASK YOUR QUESTIONS

"When will we tell our parents? How will we discipline the child? Why can't we name her Ruby? What does placenta previa mean?"

There's a fine line that an expectant dad walks. Ask too many questions or push too hard and you'll likely trigger a meltdown of one flavor or another. Ask too little or seem disinterested and you'll spend nine months in a regular state of confusion and anxiety.

WHEN WILL WE TELL OUR PARENTS? WHAT DOES PLACENTA PREVIA MEAN? HOW WILL WE PAY FOR DAY CARE?

I chose to retreat with my questions and concerns to the internet, which gave me an abundance of information and very little insight. I chose to internalize my concerns and spent many nights staring at the ceiling. Several times during the pregnancy, I actually found myself sitting on the edge of my bed struggling to breathe.

The thing is, none of my concerns were huge. But, like death by a thousand cuts, they added up.

"What will we do about day care?" became "How will I even pay for day care?"

"What should we do about church?" became "Is my child's eternal salvation in my hands alone?"

In the moments where I allowed myself to be vulnerable and confide in Mrs. Dude and others, I found not only solace, but satisfaction in the discussion. It may not always be pleasant, but there's no time like the present to talk about the questions you have and the things that matter.

3. GET YOUR SH*T FIGURED OUT

First, let me give *my* confession. I am addicted to my work. I have horrible eating habits and am overweight. I am not an equal partner with Mrs. Dude when it comes to household chores. And these are the *least* significant of my short-comings.

Most disturbing is the fact that, because I haven't figured these things out myself, there is a high likelihood that I'll pass at least some, if not all of them, on to my daughter and son. That's a serious problem.

So, please, for you . . . and your child, GET YOUR SH*T FIGURED OUT.

This change, this baby, represents an opportunity to change life for the better. Please, please, please take advantage of it. I don't care whether you're fighting addiction, have crappy financial management skills or just need to "grow up," this baby gives you an excuse to become a better person.

IT'S LIKE A RESET BUTTON IN LIFE.

Focus on the future and on something other than yourself and you'll be amazed at what's possible. I have friends and family members who struggled with all sorts of demons. Their decisions to embrace fatherhood and become good dads have made all of the difference in their lives. Take the challenge. Make a commitment. Be a great dad and an even better person!

YOUR KID IS DEPENDING ON

YOU.

4. BUILD HER A PEDESTAL

You may think this is a metaphor.

YOU'D BE
WRONG

I am actually recommending that you harvest a large piece of marble and place her on top of it. For the nine months of pregnancy (or however long you have remaining), her name should be exalted. You shall write poems in her honor and dress her head in laurel wreaths.

I've come to believe after many "convincing conversations" with Mrs. Dude that even the most empathetic dad-to-be is simply unable to conceive of the turmoil and tumult that comes when another being takes up residence in your body cavity.

I suspect that you'll question this or disagree. Perhaps even strongly. At some point, you'll say something to your partner like "I understand" or perhaps suggest a manner to relieve her discomfort that you discovered on the internet. You'll think you're providing "I feel your pain" empathy and all she'll hear is "poor baby" sympathy.

That night, when you're googling "nearby flower shops" and "marble quarries in the United States," I want you to think of me.

5. STAY SEXY

There is one pregnancy topic that is treated as virtually taboo. Yet no guide for new dads would be complete without a mention of sex.

I have no personal advice, wisdom or anecdotes to offer here.

NONE. ZIP. ZERO.

To offer any would be to overlook the fact that I failed greatly in this area. Morning sickness and a touch of moodiness (from both of us) were all I needed to put a "privacy please" placard on my bedroom door early in the pregnancy.

The one piece of reconnaissance that I will share from my informal, unscientific poll of new dads and my own experience is that *staying sexy* is much easier than *bringing sexy back*.

To be clear, this doesn't mean sex. Just sexy, my friend. Know the difference, communicate with your partner and you'll be golden.

6. LEARN THE LANGUAGE.

Colostrum. Good.

Lanugo. Neutral.

Eclampsia. Bad.

One of the greatest gifts I gave to myself during my transition from dude to dad was learning the language of pregnancy and childbirth. I created a simple game that I called "Terrifying Pregnancy Word of The Day." I'd look up a word like striae (stretch marks), learn the definition and how to pronounce it, and repeat it loudly. Some of the words were rightfully terrifying. Other just seemed ominous.

So much of this process can seem like visiting a foreign country. Worse, you'll often be received

EPISIOTOMY

In basic terms, this is an incision in the perineum made to help your baby's melon of a head to escape the birth canal. Though it is a common medical procedure, my understanding is that "episiotomy" loosely translates to "Dad, please look away!"

15

in less than hospitable terms. You need to do everything you can in advance to ensure that you are a full participant in the arrival of your child. Part of this is being able to understand and speak without hesitation.

It may seem insignificant now, but in the midst of childbirth you'll be glad you know the difference between an episiotomy and afterbirth. Though I recommend looking away for both.

7. IDENTIFY YOUR ALLIES

As a culture, we tend to treat pregnancy as an illness. We surround our mothers with a team of doctors whose goal is primarily to prevent catastrophic events. At best, we provide the mother and child with a team focused on their well-being. I have found very few examples where the dad is considered in the support planning.

As a result, I believe this to be a primary element of the father's successful transition from dude to dad. Find a small group of people that will commit to watching out for your well-being. You wouldn't show up at a wedding without a best man and some groomsmen; why would you approach the birth of your child with any less support?

I was fortunate to have a Dude to Dad wingman named Mike that was first class. Somewhere in the haze of the first night of labor, I texted him and asked that he go pick up a Double Big Mac. While this apparently exists in Egypt, Japan, and a couple other exotic lands, it doesn't exist in the United States as far as I can tell. I'd never had one, but in the moment I had failed to realize that. I'd find out later that Mike went to McDonald's and convinced them that the mythical sandwich was a matter of life-or-death. All I knew at the time, as he was arguing with the drive-thru attendant at 11:00 p.m., was that *I* was well taken care of.

Providing a support system for you in no way diminishes or distracts the focus from the mother and baby. It simply provides the assurance that you will be cared for as well, allowing you to stay focused on mom and baby. A happy dad is a helpful dad, even if his requests might be . . .

RIDICULOUS.

8. KNOW THE TEAM

I'll never forget the day after my daughter was born. As I slowly woke up, I could hear a man in the room speaking in hushed, reassuring tones about what a beautiful baby I had. I confess that for a long moment I thought that it might be a sort of divine appointment.

However, as my eyes adjusted and the fog lifted, I realized that the man in the room was my daughter's new doctor. We had met in the past with my own health needs, but this new responsibility, for both of us, made his presence seem more significant.

So much of pregnancy care is filled with private, latex glove-laden visits between doctors, midwives, and mothers. It's hard, beyond ultrasounds and emergencies, to know where we fit into the baby visits.

Despite the awkwardness of elbow-deep examinations, it is critical to know and trust the support team that surrounds the birth process. Your inner sanctum may never be examined by the individual, but you need to trust that their commitment is to the health and well-being of your growing family and not their desire to avoid lawsuits.

You don't need to attend every pelvic exam and Pap smear to feel comfortable, but you should meet your doctor, midwife, or doula well before the due date to ensure that everyone is comfortable with the team for the big day.

9. RECOGNIZE YOUR ROLE

The hardest part about writing this book is recognizing that no two pregnancies, births or parenting situations are exactly the same. You may be planning with a wife, partner, birth mom or some other perfectly wonderful individual or group.

YOU NEED TO TRUST THAT THEIR COMMITMENT IS TO THE HEALTH AND WELL-BEING OF YOUR GROWING FAMILY.

As a result, it is very hard to provide general words of insight about what role you should play through your transition from Dude to Dad.

Mine was unique in its own special way. In my struggle to manage the process, I became the recorder for the pregnancy. Through videos, blog posts, and tweets, I inventoried and reported on all aspects of the adventure from the first kick to the assembly of the crib and everything else in between. In a stage where my wife retreated into

SEEK
OPPORTUNITIES

her body's changes, I expressed my love by sharing our joy with the world. It gave me a sense of place in my marriage and in the pregnancy when everything was changing.

This sense of place and purpose is the role that an expectant father should pursue. Don't assume that your role is simply to support. Don't expect that you can "fix" things during the pregnancy. Simply seek opportunities to engage and express yourself, your feelings, and your emotions in a significant and genuine way.

TO ENGAGE AND EXPRESS YOURSELF.

10. SCHEDULE SHORT SABBATICALS

I know the Dude to Dad Doubt Spiral well.

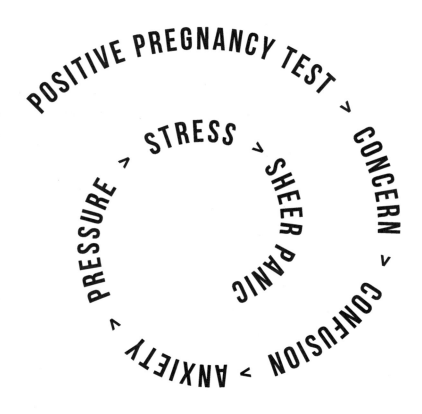

POSITIVE PREGNANCY TEST > CONCERN > CONFUSION > ANXIETY > PRESSURE > STRESS > SHEER PANIC

During this time of transition and chaos, we find ways to make the situation even more stressful by working more and sleeping less. The infinite requests and curious cravings may have been understandable and even "cute" early in the pregnancy. However, by the end, you come to believe that one more midnight run for milk-shakes may put you over the edge. While I do believe it is a time to prepare (and don't forget the pedestal!), I also believe pregnancy is a perfect time to be still and rest.

Now, please understand, I don't believe in the common logic that you should "sleep while you can" or "enjoy life before the baby comes." This is just plain foolish.

DELUSIONAL, REALLY.

When the blessed child arrives, you're going to get tired. No amount of banking sleep will help. And I've come to believe that life really begins after your child arrives.

However, research in self-control does tell us something about will power and patience that may be helpful. These aspects of self-discipline are in an exhaustible, but thankfully renewable, supply.

The lesson?

CUT YOURSELF A BREAK.

Take some time off. Skip a run. Eat a doughnut. Sleep in.

You are spending all of your willpower and strength on so many things. The only way to ensure that you'll have the right amount left is to take a break. Schedule some time just for you.

Sounds selfish? Certainly. Will it make you a better pregnancy partner? Absolutely.

FUNDUS

Though once confused by Mrs. Dude for the cake frosting called fondant, the fundus is the top of the uterus and is regularly checked before and after pregnancy to determine growth and position of the uterus.

11. PRACTICE? PRACTICE.

Practice? You're talking about practice?

One of the greatest misconceptions I had about parenting was that it was something that you should learn entirely on the fly. Build the airplane in the air. Learn on the job. Take it as it comes.

Until late in my wife's pregnancy, I generally joked my way through the process putting diapers on stuffed monkeys and testing out the breast pump. It wasn't arrogance and I definitely cared, but I was genuinely scared to death and didn't know what I didn't know.

Then, a month before my daughter arrived, I sat with my sister and nephew as he packed his birthday cake into every crack and crevice of his body. My sister, in a moment of clarity, encouraged *me* to clean him up. This immediately led to questions I'd never considered.

How do I remove the diaper while holding my cake-covered nephew?

What temperature should the water be?

How do I hold him up, rinse the soap from his hair and . . .

COULD HE JUST STOP CRYING?!

Finally, his tears and terror convinced his mother to intervene, but I had learned a valuable lesson: practice. I hear you. You have things to do. You're a franchise player in this family.

BUT, YES, I'M TALKING ABOUT PRACTICE.

12. REINVENT RITES OF PASSAGE

You are about to go through one of the most important transitions in a person's life. Seriously. No exaggeration.

Birth, death, and parenthood may be our few remaining natural transitions of importance. However, we have removed all of the necessary rituals to celebrate these transitions. We have

PERINEUM

Well, 'taint your front side and it 'taint your back side, but it's everything in between. Please see *Episiotomy* (p.11) for its role in delivery.

more rituals to mark the beginning of the football season than we do your journey from Dude to Dad.

It's time to reinvent our parental rite of passage.

- How do you want to celebrate the news that you are pregnant?

- How will you share the news with your family and friends?

- Do you want to know the sex in advance and how do you want to find out?

- How will you mark the final trimester and the end of your marriage without children?

- How would you like your child's birth to be shared with family and friends?

- Do you want family and friends visiting immediately or do you need a week to settle in?

It's been my experience that many of these things happen or pass without note or significance. We wait until three months have passed to share our pregnancy, but we're not exactly sure why. We join the latest craze (are gender cakes still a thing?) or simply find out the gender because we can, but not because we've considered the significance in our lives.

Finally, so much planning is put into place for the birth plan, but not the way we engage after the birth. Some close friends of ours made a decision not to share any news until they had over a

MAKE IT MATTER.

day with their newborn. No tweeted announcements of labor or email updates. Simply radio silence until they settled in. Beautiful.

I, on the other hand, chose to live tweet the birth, sharing each push and phase with the world. When my daughter emerged, hundreds had been following for hours. And when we shared her birth, it was a shared experience across at least four continents. Equally as beautiful.

Figure out what works for you, but make it intentional. Make it matter. Make it a rite of passage.

MAKE IT A RITE OF PASSAGE.

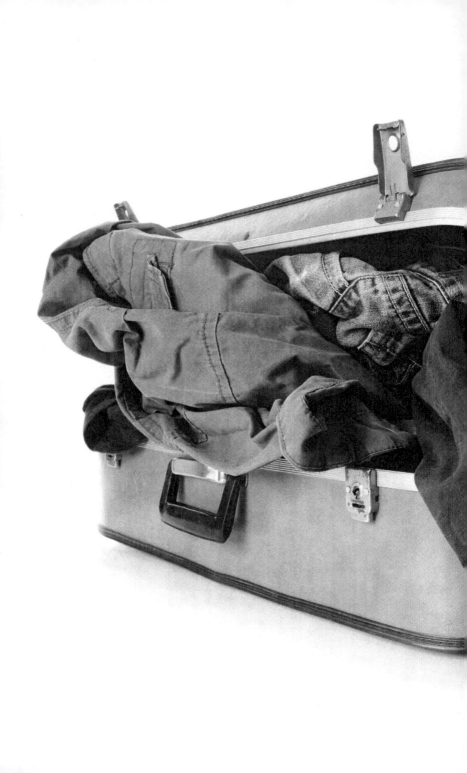

13. BE PREPARED

This is more than the Boy Scout motto and is not to be overlooked.

On the day my wife was induced, the bags had been packed for weeks, the lists of contacts were made, and the nursery prepared. All of the "important things" were in the car and we were simply waiting.

Yet, I was far from prepared.

We received a call while at the grocery store that my wife, two weeks overdue, had been squeezed in and should be at the hospital in an hour.

In short, I panicked.

I stood in the aisle of a grocery store and insisted that we should continue with our plans for the day (primarily eating cupcakes) and go into the hospital the following week. They couldn't expect us to come in "last minute" and I, for one, had no intention of having a baby that day.

In a moment of clarity, Mrs. Dude was gracious but firm. She assured me that we were ready and the time was now. The cart and cupcakes were left in the aisle as we rushed to the hospital.

While I had prepared all of the "important things," I had not taken the time to prepare myself. It may sound like new age silliness, but I think all it would have taken was a couple deep cleansing breaths to recognize that I was prepared. Thank goodness for Mrs. Dude.

Take the time to get your head straight. Go for a walk. Take a nap. Take some deep breaths.

BE
PREPARED.

"A GRAND ADVENTURE IS ABOUT TO BEGIN."

—Winnie The Pooh

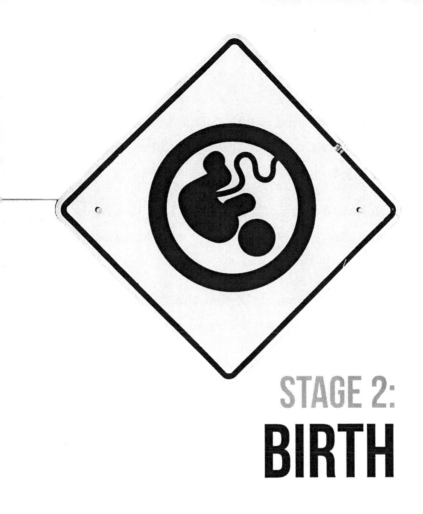

STAGE 2:
BIRTH

Wow. We're close. Very close.

But as the popular expression goes, "Close only counts in horseshoes and hand grenades," and this is no time to pick up a hobby.

You're going to need to focus like you've never focused before, because a mistake during the birth of your child will be the kind of story that your partner trots out at dinner parties for the rest of your life.

"This reminds me of the time that Hugh was out in the parking lot eating a Double Big Mac while I was in labor . . ."

"This reminds me of the time that I was giving birth and Hugh was tweeting all of his @dudeto-dad friends all night long . . ."

"This reminds me of the time that Hugh made jokes about the woman down the hall sounding like a sick donkey as I was entering hard labor . . ."

Trust me, they'll never go away.

Best option: stay focused . . .

READ ON.

1. BURN THE BABY BOOKS

I'm serious. Burn them all. Roast some marshmallows. Enjoy the warmth.*

Baby books have this not-so-subtle way of making parents feel like they are deficient or that their children are falling behind. On the flip side, they can give you a sense that you are the best parent on the planet and have a child of superior intelligence and ability.

*EDITOR'S NOTE

Dude to Dad is not a 'baby book.' It's a 'Dad book.' As such, we'd recommend that you keep it, treasure it, give it a place of honor, or pass it on to another friend when you've memorized it.

I'M SERIOUS. BURN THEM ALL.

Both of these are bad.

Parenting and childhood should not be competitive endeavors.

There are no timelines or finish lines.

The only thing that knowing these milestones and measurements will do is make you neurotic. Honestly.

Why is my child's head bigger than 95% of children?

Does the fact that my child is crawling weeks before the timeline in the book mean that I should be saving for Harvard?

My child only knows three words and *most* children know 10 at this age . . . "Honey, can you say 'tree' . . . not 'twee?' Say 'tree,' honey."

Burn them.*

Then send the pictures to babybooks@dudeto-dad.com and we'll post them for the world to see.

*EDITOR'S NOTE, PART II

We are generally very opposed to the idea of burning books. However, this time we make an exception. Burn, baby, burn.

2. INDULGE YOURSELF

All birth experiences are different. Perhaps yours will go quickly. Perhaps not. Perhaps you won't even be in the room.

Either way, there's going to be some downtime. There's going to be some just sitting around time. (Whatever you do, do NOT describe it to your wife this way.)

During this time, it's best to have something to keep you busy.

Chances are good that your partner has loaded a bag with her favorite socks, a *People* magazine, and an iPod full of soothing tunes.

NONE OF THIS IS FOR YOU.

You're going to need to prepare to indulge your-self.

Pack a bag.

SERIOUSLY.

Include something to read, something to watch and something to listen to.

Throw in some snacks (though you may want to eat these out of eye sight of your laboring partner) and some change for a soda or cup of coffee.

If you don't want to look like Richard Nixon in early photographs, throw in a disposable razor and a toothbrush. If you're spending the night, bring some heavy socks or slippers. Sleeping on a short couch isn't easy, but it's easier if you're comfortable.

Just make sure that your needs are met. You're about to become a Dad.

TREAT YOURSELF ACCORDINGLY.

SOMETHING TO READ

TOOTHBRUSH

DUDE T

SOMETHING TO WATCH

SOMETHING TO LISTEN TO

SNACKS & CHANGE

DISPENSABLE RAZOR

HEAVY SOCKS OR SLIPPERS

3. NO TIME FOR STANDUP COMEDY*

. . . or a history lesson . . . or global context.

This means that throwing your hands in the air and shouting a triumphant "thrrrreeeeee!" after the fifth pelvic exam isn't going to be met with a high five. (Sadly, because it was hilarious.)

It means that the enthralling story about American neurologist James Leonard Corning's decision to conduct the first epidural by injecting cocaine into the spine of a male in 1885 will not be acknowledged by a thoughtful nod. (This is true.)

James Leonard Corning. Nice guy.

Finally, it means that sharing family stories of giving birth in cars, your mother's six child-births being "drug free" or a kind reminder that "women have been giving birth for centuries and it is soooo natural" will not be saluted for being worldly.

It means, shut up. It's for your own health.

*As a side note, although it's no time for joking on your part, the drugs may make your partner hilarious. In her finest moment, Mrs. Dude rolled over, still asleep, and said, "What do you get when you mix an elephant and a rhino? El-eph-ino."

4. KNOW THE PLAYING FIELD

The discussions of birth plans and questions of natural births are going to be left to all of those other baby books . . . which you've burned. Shoot. I'm sure your partner has that covered.

The most important thing for you to know as you enter the birth and delivery space is where things are located.

How do you get the attention of nurses?

Where can you find ice chips?

Where does extended family wait (if they're invited)?

Which way is the parking lot?

This can be solved by a simple tour in advance. Or it can be learned the hard way.

Our "hard way" included Mrs. Dude's brother walking in the room as she was mounted in the stirrups exposed in all of her glory. Those are memories that can't be erased for any of us.

Take the tour.

BLOODY SHOW

This is either the Discovery Channel episodes that you'll watch as your wife labors away, or the light passage of blood near the end of the pregnancy. Don't worry, it's natural either way!

Your role in the miracle of birth is hard to predict. I served as 1/3 historian, 1/3 left leg holder, and 1/3 trying not to make jokes to mask my panic.

While my role wasn't clear, one thing that did become apparent quickly is that

THERE WAS NOTHING FOR ME TO FIX.

It may be a gross generalization, but at least in my family, men are the fixers.

Now, I don't mean this literally in my case. I'm not allowed around power tools. But figuratively, my role (and the role of generations of men before me) has been the role of problem solver.

This role is useless in the birthing room. There's literally nothing to fix.

AND I WOULDN'T RECOMMEND BREAKING SOMETHING TO CHANGE THIS.

6. PAMPER HER

We recommended a marble pedestal for your partner in Stage 1, but it's just silly to expect a woman to give birth on a pedestal.

In Stage 2, our recommendation is pampering. Up close and personal.

PAM·PER (VERB):

To cater excessively to someone or to her desires or feelings.

Even if you blew it for nine months of pregnancy, now is the time to shine.

Ice chips? You got it!

Foot rub? You bet!

A back issue of *Good Housekeeping* from the car? No problem.

Make it happen for your partner over the next several hours and you'll have your dadhood off to a flying start. Keep her awake through the night due to excessive keyboard clicking as you update your @dudetodad friends, and, well, we know how that ends up.

Having said all of this, you need to have a willing partner. After several hours of my best pampering, Mrs. Dude established some rules.

My tweet from that moment:

"Ok, we have now instituted a no-touching and no "are you ok?" question asking policy . . . you've been warned." @hughweber, 3/29/09, 12:20 a.m.

You have been warned.

7. BE AWARE OF THE CURVEBALL

This is where things get tricky.

No time for stand up. Uh-huh.

There's nothing to fix. Understood.

Pamper your partner. Check.

CURVEBALL!

"There was a time, I thought in my head, this is worse than dying. And I was sick of all the reassuring calm talk." —Mia, Dude

I missed the curveball. I was so focused on pampering and not fixing that I missed it. My wife isn't terribly subtle and that moment where she thought about dying was surely accompanied by a look and some sort of sigh. And I missed it.

To avoid the same mistake, you need to be alert. You need to be observant. There are no points for asking if your partner is "ok." Just be ready to respond.

It's easy to get caught up in the moment. But don't do it. The curveball is always

RIGHT AROUND THE CORNER.

8. HAVE THE RIGHT EQUIPMENT

In the midst of all of the excitement and nervousness of childbirth, the number one question that is asked about the birth process is "what should I bring to the hospital?"

So much thought is given to iPod playlists, special lighting, "take home clothes," and other nonsense, when these are clearly nice but not completely necessary.

Beyond your personal indulgence bag, there are really only four necessities. And, in the world of smart phones, three of these may all be the same device.

BREECH BIRTH

If the vaginal canal was a slide, this would be the safe and preferred way to arrive into the world. Since the vagina is in no way a slide, this feet first arrival can be filled with complications. Chances are good that your doctor or midwife will try to turn this baby around.

PHONE AND CHARGER

The birth of your child is no time to be caught with an unavailable or unusable phone.

CAMERA AND CHARGER

This isn't the time for you to develop your directing chops, but it is time to catch the moments of the miracles that exist in the hour after the birth.

LIST OF FAMILY AND FRIEND PHONE NUMBERS

The only thing worse than being without a phone is not being able to call your father-in-law or special aunt to share the news.

Finally, the only truly essential equipment is

AN INFANT CAR SEAT*

It's rarely included on the fantasy lists shared online and is truly the only thing you'll need to take your baby home.

So, do some research on the options that exist. Take the time to make sure it fits in your vehicle. Install it in advance if you can. But don't forget it.

*AUTHOR'S NOTE

We don't want to play favorites, but when Baby Dudes and Dudettes ride home from the hospital, they ride in the safe and stylish Graco car seats.**

**AUTHOR'S NOTE, PART II

Yes, that was a shameless plug for sponsorship. Baby needs a new pair of shoes . . . and a new car seat.

9. PLANS ARE WORTHLESS

Mrs. Dude is a planner. She had a pretty clear birth plan. Chances are good that she had a plan for her plan.

Now, in the original plan, I believe I was supposed to encourage her to stick with the plan. That was a silly plan.

Seven minutes into labor,

THE PLANS WERE THROWN OUT.

To be clear, it's important to discuss these things. It's important to ask the questions and get answers.

As former President, General and Dad, Dwight Eisenhower once said, "Plans are worthless. Planning is everything."

Your role is to support the plan with all of your moral, ethical and physical strength and then to develop selective amnesia and fully abandon it when it's clear that your partner has evolved in her thinking and the situation has changed.

Being a stickler for the plan isn't safe.

BE SAFE.

VERNIX

When I first heard it, it made me think of spring. When I first saw it, it made me think of cheese. When I first got it on my shirt, well, I gagged a little. This coating on a newborn's skin helps it slip 'n slide its way down the birth canal.

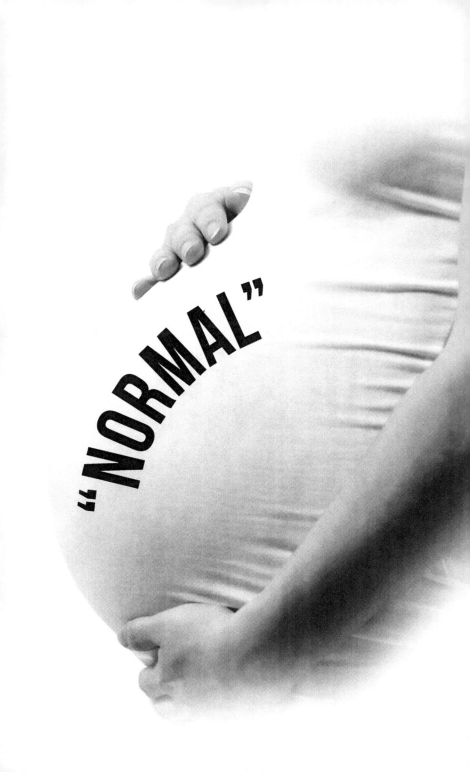

10. KNOW THE RULES AND NOBODY GETS HURT

I had some pretty big assumptions as I approached my daughter's birth.

I assumed that there were some pretty standard procedures and that the doctors would make the decisions. I was along for the ride and didn't have a voice in the process.

I assumed that birth experiences were either good and "normal" or complicated and likely Cesarean. I didn't recognize the broad spectrum of birth experiences.

I assumed that people went to hospitals because pregnancy needed to be treated like an illness or disease. I hadn't considered that giving birth was natural and not medical.

Plain and simple, I didn't know the rules. I didn't know that advocating for my partner was a responsibility and a privilege. I didn't know that the monitors and traditional methods were optional and often unnecessary.

I was anxious for much of the labor, concerned about the health of my wife and my baby, and thankful for nearby medical support. However, I was also thankful for the sense of peace we claimed in our delivery room. I was thankful for the voice that Mrs. Dude and I had in the decision-making for our birth.

This sense of peace and voice can happen in any setting. It doesn't require doulas or deep water. It simply requires knowing the rules.

AND, IN THE END, THERE ARE NO RULES.

11. OWN THE EXPERIENCE

Even in the most peaceful births, things are happening so quickly that it's easy to lose touch with the experience. You need to fight to own it.

My favorite memories from the wacky, wonderful ordeal would have been lost if I hadn't placed such importance on remembering the details.

The nurse that told Mrs. Dude that she "must have one heck of a uterus in there!" Mrs. Dude shouting, "I want the baby out before she starts getting piercings and painting her toenails." The blame for excessive flatulence being placed on her being "heavily medicated . . . medicined . . . with medicines."

MUCOUS PLUG

This is pretty straight forward. This snotty substance seals and protects the cervical canal during pregnancy. Its release into the world is a pretty good sign that a baby is on the way. I would strongly encourage against using Google images on this one.

Find a way to collect the experience. Mental snapshots, tweets, texts, and frantic notes saved the day for us. These stories have become priceless pieces of our family myth. Saving them is worth the effort.

12. BREATHE

There's a lot of breathing that happens before birth. Shallow breathing for pushing through contractions. Deep breathing so nobody passes out. Held breaths at the moment of delivery.

Take time to breathe.

You won't get a coach. Nobody is likely to suggest it . . . until you pass out.

Just breathe.

Breathe your last dude breath.

Breathe in the air of the miracles happening around you.

BREATHE...

13. DECIDE TO BE A DAD

All of this is going to happen. It's going to be unique. It's going to be personal.

In fact, there's no way to tell what your *this* will look like.

But, in the end, *this* is going to happen. You're going to be a Dad.

But there's one more very important decision to make before this happens.

You need to **decide** to be a Dad.

That's right, it sounds ridiculous, but you need to decide to be a Dad.

Oh, you're already a father. You've clearly put a check in that box already. But this is more important.

Look in the mirror. Consider it carefully. Decide.
Then, announce,

"I'M GOING TO BE A DAD."

Everything will be easier after you make this
simple, but life-changing decision.

"WATCHING YOUR HUSBAND BECOME A FATHER IS REALLY SEXY AND WONDERFUL."

—Cindy Crawford

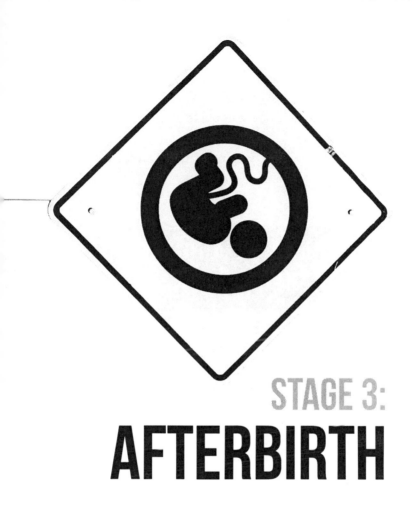

STAGE 3:
AFTERBIRTH

Congratulations! You did it.

You watched a human being emerge from another human being. Quite the accomplishment.

Unfortunately, I stretched the truth a bit in the last section when suggesting that everything would be easier once you decided to be a dad.

However, now that you're in this to win it . . . let's get to it.

1. YOU AND ME AND THE BABY MAKES THREE

Welcome to the new normal!

You will never again be able to make a single decision without considering the impact on your child.

Since the birth of my daughter, every decision is processed by considering the impact on her. This is true in use of money, use of time and prioritization of life's many scheduling conflicts.

This doesn't mean that I always make the perfect decision, but it means I consider them in light of her.

Prior to the baby, there were purchases that would be made impulsively without a consideration of impact. Prior to the baby, I worked some long nights and extended social gatherings without a handwringing thought about a waiting meal or wife. I can be honest in saying that even marriage didn't have this impact on me. (Mrs. Dude wasn't terribly excited to hear this, but it is absolutely true.)

If fathers were being completely candid, I think they would have to admit that even in their actions that are less-than-fatherly, they still consider the impact on their new and growing family.

YOU SHOULD START CONSIDERING NOW.

2. SH*T IS ABOUT TO GET REAL

Picture the worst possible imaginable disturbing (borderline criminal) thing that could be done to you by a child, increase it by several orders of magnitude, and expect it to occur weekly.

I'm going to leave out some details here. It's really for your own good. You see, my daughter had some digestive disorders in these first couple months that have required group participation in the process of waste excretion. I know this is vague language, but I can assure you— it's better that way. One of the side effects of this condition was projectile pooping. I'm talking real magic bullet sort of stuff. Imagine a world where magic poops can appear several feet from your angelic child. Chilling, horrific stuff.

In less eventful activities, my daughter has managed to project milky vomit into my ears. I have been covered from elbow to shoulder in a goop that closely resembles the most incredibly foul

CHILLING, HORRIFIC STUFF.

baby poop mixed with a liquid form of death. Most recently, she woke me up by spraying me with a gallon and a half of saltine crackers and Gatorade®.

There is nothing sweet or adorable about this. It's just a fact.

Now, I once told a prospective employer that one of my weaknesses was vomit. This immersive experience in body fluids and semi-solids is literally my worst nightmare.

But, as G. I. Joe used to say, knowing is half the battle, so I'm going to hope that this helps you in some little way.

THERE IS NOTHING SWEET OR ADORABLE ABOUT THIS.

IT'S JUST A FACT.

3. LET ME INTRODUCE YOU TO SOMEONE: YOUR WIFE

Now, it's time for some potentially unsettling news.

Remember when we talk about how "everything has changed?" That includes your partner.

Your wife at her best will be a fundamentally different person than the woman you met on your first date. Your wife at her worst will be infinitely more terrifying than the monster you imagined under your bed as a child.* Don't expect her to be who she was BC (before child).

Now, there is no judgment implied in this. Plain and simple, she's changed.

*AUTHOR'S NOTE

Mrs. Dude smiled and nodded when I shared this with her. Then, she roared a terrible roar.

I mean she did just squeeze an adorable 7–9 pound watermelon out of a stretchy but human garden hose.* Cut her some slack.

Much like you're figuring out your place in this new and emerging world, she is too.

Get to know her all over again and things will be fine.

---

*The whole watermelon/garden hose metaphor has always struck me as a strange way of explaining childbirth, but I've yet to come up with something better.

4. PARTNERS DON'T NEED PEDESTALS

Now that you're reacquainted, it's time to shake up the relationship.

This stage you're in, this "new normal," this grand adventure is a long-term situation. Your relationship needs to reflect the emerging nature of your family. You need to recognize that not

DO IT GENTLY.

only are you in this together, but that surviving and thriving will require a dynamic partnership.

There is simply no room for a pedestal in a partnership.

So, take her down. Do it gently. Do it gradually. But, return her to the same plane as you.

This doesn't mean that a magical (perhaps mythical?) *equal* partnership will result. However, by removing the pedestal, you've created an environment where the possibility exists.

It's important that I be clear about one more thing. Do not *replace* her on the pedestal with *yourself*. Are we clear?

5. CONTROL IS A MYTH

Parenting isn't a situation where MacGyver or Mr. T is going to be of any assistance to you. There are no solutions to this dilemma.

Perhaps the biggest misconception that I had coming into fatherhood was that I would somehow be able to "figure out" my child.

Oh, I knew there would be stages. I had heard about the terrible twos and teething, but I imagined that between these milestones I would figure the super-secret song or noise or funny face and that I would magically disarm the greatest of tantrums and tears.

This was incredibly misguided and now feels borderline stupid.

Any "solution" you come up with likely last about thirty minutes at best. In many cases, it only lasts about thirty seconds.

DON'T EVER GIVE UP, BUT ALSO DON'T THINK THAT YOU'RE ACTUALLY IN CONTROL.

6. FAIL FAST

Despite having the best intentions, I have filled my parenting report card with a fair number of failing grades.

Never loses temper. Fail.

Always makes daughter and son his priority. Fail.

Equal partner with his wife. Fail.

If there is a silver lining in this record of failure, it is that I've made a personal commitment to failing fast. When I make a mistake and recognize it (or have it pointed out . . . thanks Mrs. Dude!), I immediately move to correct, adapt, or apologize for it.

This isn't easy.

You'll be amazed at how regular exposure to toddler tantrums will make lying down on the floor and kicking your feet seem perfectly reasonable.

The truth is, time to time, you're going to fail.

I've taught my daughter a simple call and response that may come in handy in these times: "When things get tough . . . I try harder."

7. KNOW YOUR LIMITS

This is important.

If you don't know your limits, trust friends and family when they tell you that you've reached them.

This is not to say that we are all ticking time bombs, but I have heard too many fellow moms AND dads say through tears, "This is never going to end. I am never going to sleep. I can't handle this anymore," to believe that I am the only one.

Speaking personally, there are times (each and every day) when parenting is completely overwhelming. You are exhausted, the baby is inconsolable and the tension between you and your wife is high. Unless you learn to recognize when you just can't handle any more stress (emotionally, spiritually, physically), there is a high likelihood that you will put yourself in a position to do and say things that you wouldn't normally think possible.

SO STEP AWAY.
GET SOME SPACE.
CALL A FRIEND.

But most importantly, acknowledge that you are overwhelmed and don't take it out on your spouse or child.

8. BE FULLY PRESENT

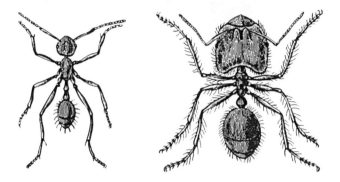

Being fascinated by ants and clouds isn't a passive exercise. Curiosity about the mundane requires commitment and control.

It's about being fully present.

As an adult and parent, we miss so many moments in the glare of our phones and computers. Bearing the full burden of responsibility for our children, we often throw ourselves into our work, ignoring the moments that are passing by in our life and for our children.

My daughter developed a very unusual habit, when she first started speaking, of repeating

herself three times. In a truly devastating moment of self-awareness, it became clear that this was repetition she often found necessary to break my attention from my iPhone or laptop.

Life can become too busy and distracted that it's easy to feel like being in the room as our kids is an acceptable form of quality time.

Being a Dad, I've come to learn the hard way, requires more than simply being physically present—it requires being fully present.

9. REJECT ROLE MODELS

Before I became a father, I saw my father and grandfather as perfect Dads.

They were always full of life and love. They demonstrated complete commitment to family and their children. They made tremendous sacrifices for the happiness of their children.

IN SHORT, THEY WERE PERFECT DAD ROLE MODELS.

I agonized in the months before my daughter's birth about how I would ever be able to measure up to the parenting of my dad. With role models, we choose to focus on the ideal qualities and successes of an individual.

The problem is, in reality, they were both just as challenged by fatherhood as we all are.

My dad, a self-employed electrician, worked unreasonably long hours putting much of the demands of raising my siblings on my mom's able shoulders. My grandfather regretted waiting years to apologize for discouraging my mom from pursuing college after high school.

Neither of these diminishes their ultimate success at parenting, but they do require rethinking the negative impacts of role models.

As role models, both of these men created un-realistic expectations for me as a new dad. The standards that I imagined weren't even reached by these wonderful men. However, as normal human beings, their mistakes and challenges have reassured me that great dads come from average men like me and you.

10. TRIANGULATE

There's a process in sailing and navigation called triangulation. This ancient process involves finding three fixed points in an effort to better determine the location of your boat.

When you're feeling lost, a similar process can help you find your bearings as a dad.

To triangulate in parenting, you need to find three people.

One should be a stage ahead of you. A parent of pre-teens is perfect. They are far enough along to have some confidence and close enough to having teens that they know how little they know. They'll make sure you don't get cocky.

One should be a stage behind you. Without kids to cloud their judgment, they are overjoyed to become parents. You have something to teach them and they have something to remind you. They'll make sure you don't forget joy.

One should be in exactly the same stage. This person is most important and they need to be the honest type. They'll make sure you don't drown.

My "same stage" guy's name is Andy.

Andy loves his family, but is able to confess fully his feelings of being overwhelmed, being insecure and being exhausted. He admits to the challenges of marriage, the misgivings of parenting and mourning his lost Dude status. Andy and I don't see each other often, but our brief conversations have often kept me afloat as a Dad.

FIND YOUR ANDY.

11. CELEBRATE THE MOMENTS

I once had a friend suggest to me that parenting was like riding a bull—if you don't pay attention and commit fully, you're going to get trampled.

I had this vision of a couple rough weeks. It would take time. I would get my bumps and bruises. I'm only human after all. But when I "figured out" parenting and my daughter, I'd be a professional and life would get back to normal.

What I didn't consider about bull riding or parenting is that you usually don't get the luxury of riding the same bull twice. Each bull comes with its own unique enthusiasm for tossing you on the dirt and stepping on your chest. One week you're riding Smackdown, the next week you draw Bushwacker.* This is why

8 SECONDS

of riding is considered a successful effort.

For a parent, it might mean that one week you draw Pink Eye or Potty Training and the next week you get Pertussis or Bulging Fontanelle (which would actually make a great name for a bull!). Each has a way of reminding you how little you know and that the little you do know really doesn't matter.

Celebrate those moments of pride when the little thing you did made all the difference. But,

*Note: Bushwacker is a real bull with a "buck-off percentage" of 100%. Wowza.

also celebrate those times you ended up on the ground. Celebrate the confidence and wisdom that comes with falling down as a father. Repeatedly. Celebrate the understanding and patience that comes with knowing that you'll never have your kids "figured out." Nor would you want to (where's the fun in that?). Celebrate the fact that committing fully and paying attention is sometimes the most important thing you can do.

What doesn't kill you, in bull riding or parenting, probably won't make you stronger, but I believe that it will prepare you for the ride that lies ahead.

12. FREE TO BE ME

In all of this talk of focusing on wives and children, it's important to remember not to neglect the needs of another critical family member: you.

If you've accepted all of the new realities of your life (or at least a portion of those realities), you need to begin to consider who you are with and within these new expectations.

For much of my adult (and notably, single) life, travel was a critical part of my well-being and happiness. I revel in the experience of visiting a new community, meeting new people, and collecting stories to share when I return back home. With the birth of my daughter, I quickly recognized that long or frequent trips were not compatible with the kind of Dad that I wanted to be.

After some initial despair, I realized that a deeper commitment to reading was a way to experience many of these same joys. This means our home is flooded with books, magazines, and

EVERYTHING HAS CHANGED.

TIME

HOBBIES

FINANCES

newspapers. Every Sunday, my daughter and I share the ritual of rushing to the front steps and grabbing the newspaper.

As we noted at the beginning, everything has changed. This will impact our hobbies, our time and our finances. Yet, we need to be certain that our passions and dreams aren't completely dis-regarded and left behind.

By paying attention to these needs, you will be a happier individual and hopefully a better Dad.

13. RAISE A CHILD OF POSSIBILITY

Early in my Dude to Dad transition, my good friend Scott suggested to me that my one and only responsibility as a dad was to help my kid become the best possible version of themselves.

It's so easy to see a world-class athlete in the throwing motion of a three-year-old or the next pop star in the world's most adorable version of "Twinkle, Twinkle, Little Star." It's even easier to hope that they'll grow up to embrace the same passions and professions that you hold.

It's a much, much harder task to raise a child of possibility who sees nothing but opportunity in every moment and support from you in every adventure.

This isn't to suggest indulgence or excess in parenting. It's simply to say, let them ripen a bit. Let them explore and experience life. Let them fail, perhaps even spectacularly.

But let them do all of this in an environment where these things are ok.

One day they may grow up and write a book just to thank you. Perhaps they will discover or create or experience something fantastic.

Perhaps they'll be happy and fulfilled and the best possible version of themselves.

"IT IS A WISE

KNOWS HIS

FATHER THAT OWN CHILD."

—Shakespeare

And in the end . . . the love you take is equal to the love you make. So, make sure they know your love.

Because, in the end, that's all that matters.

EPILOGUE

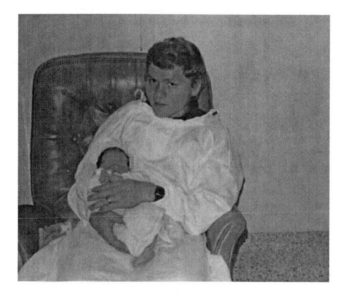

This is a picture I've always loved of my dad. He is all of eighteen years old, sitting in an overstuffed chair in a hospital gown, holding me on my first day.

He looks even younger than he is. He looks more confident than he possibly could have been.

The thing I always focused on is the placement of his hands. He's not supporting me from underneath. He appears to be embracing me. I was clearly placed in his arms. Entrusted. And he was going to do everything in his power to make sure he didn't let me down.

I'm confident that my dad didn't read any books before my birth and his dad wouldn't have been much help either. I imagine that he set out with the simple hopes we all do—he wanted to be the best dad possible. He wanted to help that baby he was entrusted with become the person he was meant to be.

This book may not have the answers. It simply hopes to provide some things to consider.

And, in the end, perhaps it's all really just a thank you to the eighteen-year-old in the picture who has given so much to me.

YES, PLEASE USE IT!

#dudetodad

NOTE:

Writing a book usually implies one of two things:

Demonstrated expertise about the subject matter gained through research, study, and a body of academic work.

Accumulation of a lifetime of experiences worthy of adoration or imitation.

I've earned no degrees in parenting or childhood development. My three-year-old has survived the first couple years, but my parenting can't be described as anything better than a C+ (the plus is for the sincere effort—dedicated and determined).

Despite that, I believe that every parent has something to share, including me.

I'd love to help you to share your parenting wisdom as well. Feel free to use #dudetodad on Twitter or email ideas for guest posts or shared content to dad@dudetodad.com.

THANKS

This project was the brainchild of Christopher Robbins and the team at Familius. Despite crazy schedules and a short writing timelines, it was Mrs. Dude that concluded that this was simply an opportunity that we couldn't say no to. The patience and partnership that I see from Familius are a clear indication that this relationship is just getting started.

My "Dude Wingman" and close friend, Mike Billeter, deserves credit for his immediate enthusiasm for the project and his ongoing counsel on all matters of substance and grammar. I am eternally grateful for his assistance and friendship.

I've learned so much about children, parenting, and family from Scott Friesen, Sara Sommervold, Zach Hamilton, and Bobby and June George. The roots of my parenting are found in the basement of the Friesen household, over cups of coffee at Queen City Bakery, and at the office of Baan Dek Montessori. Thanks friends.

I'm blessed with a family filled with an incredible variety of parenting examples to draw from. I'm surrounded by plentiful aunts, uncles, and cousins galore, but I want to especially acknowledge my brothers, sister, and in-laws. Luke and Mandy, Adam and Becky, Becca and Seth, Justin, and Jennifer, I appreciate you more than you know. You provided shining examples and cautionary tales that have become important parts of all of the parenting that Mrs. Dude and I do.

Mom and Dad, you've set the standard for something remarkable. You raised me (and my siblings) as a child of possibility and the true rewards of your parenting are being realized through the love of your kids and your bounty of grandchildren. Congratulations on a job well done.

Finally, and most importantly, I thank Mrs. Dude (aka my lovely wife, Amy). Whether it was sharing her breast pump or putting up with having the class clown as her partner in birth classes, she has parented with grace and consistency. She sacrifices without stumbling, loves without condition, and apparently has one heck of a uterus.

NOTE FOR EMERSON AND FINN

I'm certain that there are decisions that I will make, actions that I will take, and things that I will say in the coming years that will make so much of this Dude to Dad wisdom seem foolish or downright hypocritical.

Just know that as I write this and forever more, I believe you are a miracle. I believe you sit at the starting line of a lifetime of infinite possibility.

Unconditionally and eternally, I am proud of you and I love you.

Yours,

Dad

TERRIFYING PREGNANCY WORDS OF THE DAY

For your sake, and your wife's utter amusement, the Terrifying Pregnancy Words of the Day are collected here.

BLOODY SHOW

This is either the Discovery Channel episodes that you'll watch as your wife labors away, or the light passage of blood near the end of the pregnancy. Don't worry, it's natural either way!

BREECH BIRTH

If the vaginal canal was a slide, this would be the safe and preferred way to arrive into the world. Since the vagina is in no way a slide, this feet first arrival can be filled with complications. Chances are good that your doctor or midwife will try to turn this baby around.

EPISIOTOMY

In basic terms, this is an incision in the perineum made to help your baby's melon of a head to escape the birth canal. Though it is a common medical procedure, my understanding is that "episiotomy" loosely translates to "Dad, please look away!"

FUNDUS

Though once confused by Mrs. Dude for the cake frosting called fondant, the fundus is the top of the uterus and is regularly checked before and after pregnancy to determine growth and position of the uterus.

MUCOUS PLUG

This is pretty straight forward. This snotty substance seals and protects the cervical canal during pregnancy. Its release into the world is a pretty good sign that a baby is on the way. I would strongly encourage against using Google images on this one.

PERINEUM

Well, 'taint your front side and it 'taint your back side, but it's everything in between. Please see *Episiotomy* for its role in delivery.

VERNIX

When I first heard it, it made me think of spring. When I first saw it, it made me think of cheese. When I first got it on my shirt, well, I gagged a little. This coating on a newborn's skin helps it slip 'n slide its way down the birth canal.

ABOUT HUGH WEBER

Hugh Weber started DudetoDad.com as a genuine cry for help from an ordinary dude who wanted to be an extraordinary dad. He is currently in the third year of his Dude to Dad transition and lives in the 'OTA states with Mrs. Dude, his daughter Emerson, and his son Finn.

ABOUT FAMILIUS

Welcome to a place where mothers are celebrated, not compared. Where heart is at the center of our families, and family at the center of our homes. Where boo boos are still kissed, cake beaters are still licked, and mistakes are still okay. Welcome to a place where books—and family—are beautiful. Familius: a book publisher dedicated to helping families be happy.

Familius was founded in 2012 with the intent to align the founders' love of publishing and family with the digital publishing renaissance which occurred simultaneously with the Great Recession. The founders believe that the traditional family is the basic unit of society, and that a society is only as strong as the families that create it. Familius's mission is to help families be happy. We invite you to participate with us in strengthening your family by being part of the Familius family. Go to www.familius.com to subscribe and receive information about our books, articles, and videos.

Website: www.familius.com
Facebook: www.facebook.com/paterfamilius
Twitter: @familiustalk, @paterfamilius1
Pinterest: www.pinterest.com/familius